FASCINATING FACTS

HISTORY

BY M. J. YORK

I WANT YOU
FOR U.S. ARMY
NEAREST RECRUITING STATION

JUV NONFIC
909 YOR

Published by The Child's World®
1980 Lookout Drive • Mankato, MN 56003-1705
800-599-READ • www.childsworld.com

Photographs ©: iStockphoto, cover (Genghis Khan), 1 (Genghis Khan), 2, 3, 4, 5, 8, 10, 12–13, 18, 20–21 (right), 24, back cover (bottom); Everett Historical/Shutterstock Images, cover (Uncle Sam), 1 (Uncle Sam), 9, 12, 14, 16; Shutterstock Images, cover (*Titanic*), 1 (*Titanic*), 11, 16–17; Svetlana Foote/Shutterstock Images, cover (bear), 1 (bear), 15; Repina Valeriya/Shutterstock Images, cover (pyramid), 1 (pyramid), 6; Keith Lance/iStockphoto, 7, back cover (top); Steve Estvanik/Shutterstock Images, 19; Everett - Art/Shutterstock Images, 20; Michael Burrell/iStockphoto, 20–21 (left)

ISBN 9781503844605 (Reinforced Library Binding)
ISBN 9781503846258 (Portable Document Format)
ISBN 9781503847446 (Online Multi-user eBook)
LCCN 2019957939

Printed in the United States of America

ABOUT THE AUTHOR

M. J. York is a children's author and editor living in Minnesota. She loves learning about all kinds of fascinating facts.

CONTENTS

Caligula.

4

History is the story of our shared past. It includes the grand, important events we learn about in school. And it tells of the famous people who made a big impact to create the world as we know it.

Caligula.

But history is also found in the oddball, the quirky, and the downright weird. Sometimes the timing of history can be surprising. Events may have happened when we would not have expected them to.

Ordinary people do unusual things in their daily lives. And history's movers and shakers have human quirks behind their grand actions. Many weird things have happened during wartime. And U.S. history is full of oddities, too.

From Emperor Caligula's favorite horse to the Australian army's war against emus, take a trip through some of history's most fascinating facts.

CHAPTER ONE

It Happened When?

Humans have recorded history for only 5 percent of the years they have been around. The earliest known writing was about 5,000 years ago. But modern humans have been around for 100,000 years.

◄ Queen Cleopatra of Egypt was closer in time to the moon landing than to the building of the pyramids. She was born in 69 BC. Humans walked on the moon about 2,000 years later. The Pyramids of Giza were built about 2,500 years before her time.

The moon landing happened so soon after the first airplane flight that the first person to fly a plane was alive at the same time as the first person to walk on the moon.

In 2015, Great Britain finished paying off its debt from ending slavery in 1833. The government paid slaveholders when it freed enslaved people. It spent 40 percent of its annual budget, which today would be more than $3 billion.

▲

The Fourth of July is famous as America's birthday. But it is not actually the day the Declaration of Independence was signed. Congress voted for independence on July 2, 1776. The document was approved on July 4. It was not signed until August 2.

CHAPTER TWO

History's Unusual Leaders

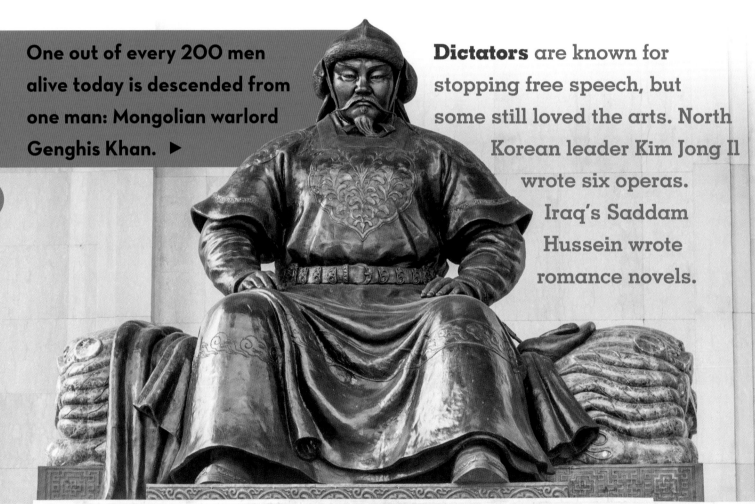

One out of every 200 men alive today is descended from one man: Mongolian warlord Genghis Khan. ▶

Dictators are known for stopping free speech, but some still loved the arts. North Korean leader Kim Jong Il wrote six operas. Iraq's Saddam Hussein wrote romance novels.

8

Roman emperor Caligula ordered his army to attack the ocean. He wanted to defeat Neptune, god of the sea. He had the soldiers collect seashells as prizes of war. Caligula also wanted to make his horse a **consul**, but the ruler was murdered first.

Mexican leader Santa Anna lost the same leg twice. He lost a leg in battle and gave it a fancy funeral. But when the people got mad at him, they dug it up and dragged it through the streets. He also lost his fake leg. The U.S. Army took it during a battle. It is found today in a museum in Illinois.

Charles VI of France thought he was made of glass. He suffered from a mental condition called the glass delusion. It is said that he wrapped himself in blankets so he would not break.

Mansa Musa of Mali was the richest person ever. He traveled through Egypt in 1325. He spent so much gold in the country that he ruined the economy there for a decade.

The youngest king in history was crowned before he was born in the year AD 309. Shah Shapur II led the Sassanian Empire in Persia from birth. Legend says the empire's **nobles** put the crown on his mother's belly.

One of the longest-ruling kings was also one of the youngest. King Sobhuza II of Swaziland ruled for 82 years. That is the longest reign in history that is dated reliably. In 1899, he took the throne when he was just four months old.

10

The longest-ruling family in history heads Japan today. The same **dynasty** has led Japan for 2,600 years.

The Imperial Palace in Tokyo is home to the ruling family of Japan.

CHAPTER THREE

These Unique United States

The first African in America was looking for the fountain of youth. Juan Garrido was a **conquistador** with the explorer Juan Ponce de León. Later, Garrido went searching for the Fountain of Youth in Florida.

◀ Uncle Sam was a real person. Samuel Wilson packed meat in barrels for soldiers in the War of 1812 (1812–1815). He stamped the barrels with "U.S." for United States. But the soldiers called the food "Uncle Sam's." Later, a cartoonist made Uncle Sam a famous symbol for the U.S. government.

12

In 1918, Woodrow Wilson was the first sitting president to cross the Atlantic Ocean.

The current 50-star U.S. flag was designed by a high school student. In 1958, Robert Heft's teacher had the class design flags. Heft got a B minus, but the teacher said he would get an A if the flag became official. Heft sent his flag to his congressperson, and it was chosen.

13

Ohio was not an official state for 150 years. Back in 1803, Congress missed one of the steps to make Ohio a state. President Dwight D. Eisenhower signed the law fixing the mistake in 1953.

CHAPTER FOUR

War Stories

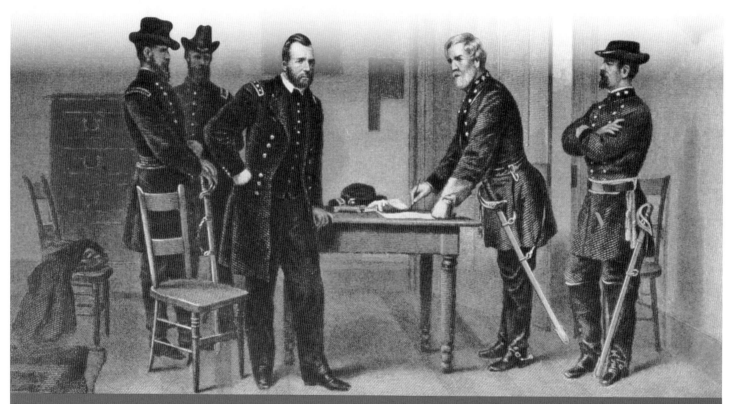

14

The bloodiest war in U.S. history began and ended at the same man's house. The First Battle of Bull Run was the first big battle of the U.S. Civil War (1861–1865). It happened in Wilmer McLean's yard. He wanted to get away from the fighting, so he moved to Appomattox, Virginia. Confederate general Robert E. Lee surrendered in McLean's new parlor.

In 1962, a bear wandered into an air force base in Minnesota, almost starting a **nuclear** war. A guard saw a shadow climbing the fence and set off the alarm. Several planes with nuclear weapons almost took off.
They were stopped just in time, when people realized a bear was the "spy."

▶

The Australian army lost a "war" against emus. The large flightless birds were ruining crops, so the government sent in troops. However, the birds were tough to kill. Troops used 2,500 bullets to kill just 200 emus. The troops soon gave up.

No one died in one of the longest wars in history, which lasted 335 years. A Dutch admiral declared war on the British Isles of Scilly in 1651. No one ever actually fought. They even forgot that they were at war. A peace treaty was finally signed in 1986.

The Swiss Army used carrier pigeons to send messages until 1994.

Adolf Hitler

In 1945, Japanese soldier Hiroo Onoda was alone in a jungle in the Philippines and did not learn that World War II (1939–1945) was over. He did not stop fighting until 1974. His former commanding officer had to meet with him in person to convince him to surrender.

▲

Adolf Hitler's nephew fought for the U.S. Navy in World War II. William Patrick Hitler also wrote an article for *Look* magazine called "Why I Hate My Uncle."

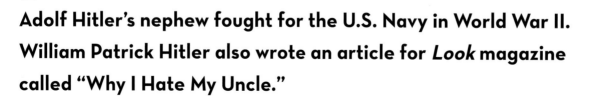

Milunka Savić disguised herself as a man so she could fight for the Serbian army in 1912. When she was found out, her commander said she could be a nurse instead. But Savić wanted to fight. The commander said he would give her an answer the next morning. Savić said she would wait, standing at attention all night. He gave in and let her keep fighting.

1912

◄ Explorer Robert Ballard found the lost ocean liner the *Titanic*, which had sunk in 1912. But he did not mean to. Ballard was actually on a secret mission for the U.S. Navy.

CHAPTER FIVE

Weird Past Lives

In the middle ages in Europe, barbers both shaved beards and pulled teeth. They also performed surgery. ▶

Ancient India's highly skilled surgeons trained by cutting into the skin of fruit. They would carefully remove the seeds. They also used dead animals to learn their craft.

18

Ancient Roman toilets sometimes exploded. The Romans' sewers were advanced for the time, but nothing stopped gases from building up in them. This caused flames to occasionally shoot out of the toilets. ▶

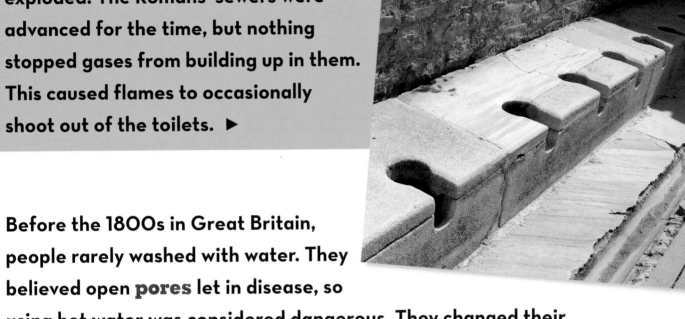

Before the 1800s in Great Britain, people rarely washed with water. They believed open **pores** let in disease, so using hot water was considered dangerous. They changed their clothes often and rubbed their skin with a dry cloth to keep from smelling.

In the early 1900s, visitors to New York's Coney Island could see a large exhibit of premature babies. The babies were in **incubators**. It was like a carnival sideshow. But it also saved the lives of many babies that likely would have died without the care. Entrance fees paid for the babies' care.

▲

During Queen Elizabeth I's reign (1558–1603), pale skin was the height of fashion. Women painted their faces white with toxic makeup made with lead. They even drew on veins to make their skin look see-through.

Food, Fashion, and Fun

In 1907, French waiters went on strike for their right to grow mustaches. Laws at the time kept lower-class men from growing them. The waiters wanted fashionable mustaches like many upper-class men. They wanted higher pay and better hours, too. ▼

In ancient China, people kept crickets as pets. About 1,000 years ago, some people even held cricket fights for entertainment. Cricket fights are still held today.

In the 1800s, artists used a shade of paint made from mummies. Called mummy brown, it was made with ground-up mummies from ancient Egyptian burials. The last manufacturer produced the paint until the 1960s.

The Hittites, an ancient people of the Middle East, may have used doughnuts in their religious services. Texts describe a special bread with a hole in it.

Glossary

conquistador (kun-KEE-stuh-dohr) A conquistador was a member of a Spanish expedition to the Americas in the 1500s, especially a mission to conquer an area. Ponce de León was a conquistador.

consul (KON-sul) A consul was the most important elected officer in ancient Rome. Caligula wanted to make his horse a consul.

delusion (di-LOO-zhuhn) A delusion is a mental illusion. The king of France had a delusion that he was made of glass.

dictators (DIK-tay-turz) Dictators are rulers who control their countries completely, usually using force. Kim Jong Il and Saddam Hussein were both dictators.

dynasty (DY-nuh-stee) A dynasty is a family that passes rule of a country from parents to children for a long period of time. A dynasty may rule for thousands of years.

economy (i-KON-uh-mee) An economy is how a country runs its money, trade, and industry. Egypt's economy was ruined.

incubators (ING-kyuh-bay-turz) Incubators are machines that provide warm, stable conditions for babies that are born early or sick. Incubators save many babies' lives.

nobles (NOH-buhlz) Nobles are members of the highest social classes, especially in kingdoms and empires. Nobles often crown new rulers.

nuclear (NOO-klee-ur) Something that is nuclear has to do with the power that comes from splitting atoms. A nuclear war would use nuclear weapons of mass destruction.

pores (PORZ) Pores are the tiny holes in skin that sweat comes out of. Washing with hot water can open the skin's pores.

surgery (SUR-jur-ee) Surgery is a medical treatment that usually involves cutting into the body. In the middle ages in Europe, barbers often performed simple surgery.

To Learn More

In the Library

Braun, Eric. *Incredible History Trivia: Fun Facts and Quizzes.*
Minneapolis, MN: Lerner Publications, 2018.

History! The Past as You've Never Seen It Before. New York, NY:
DK Publishing, 2019.

Manzanero, Paula K. *The Who Was? History of the World.*
New York, NY: Penguin Workshop, 2019.

On the Web

Visit our website for links about history:

childsworld.com/links

Note to Parents, Teachers, and Librarians: We routinely verify our Web links to make sure they are safe and active sites. So encourage your readers to check them out!

Index

24